MY 1ST BOOK OF
Seven Continents

Sara Kale

Rainbow Arts Studio
Copyright © 2022 Sara Kale
All Rights Reserved

Amazon Page : amazon.com/author/sarakale
Email : sara.rainbowartsstudio@gmail.com
IG : rainbow_artsstudio

What are Continents?

Continents are vast expanses of land, separated by oceans. Earth has seven continents: Asia, Africa, North America, South America, Antartica, Europe and Australia

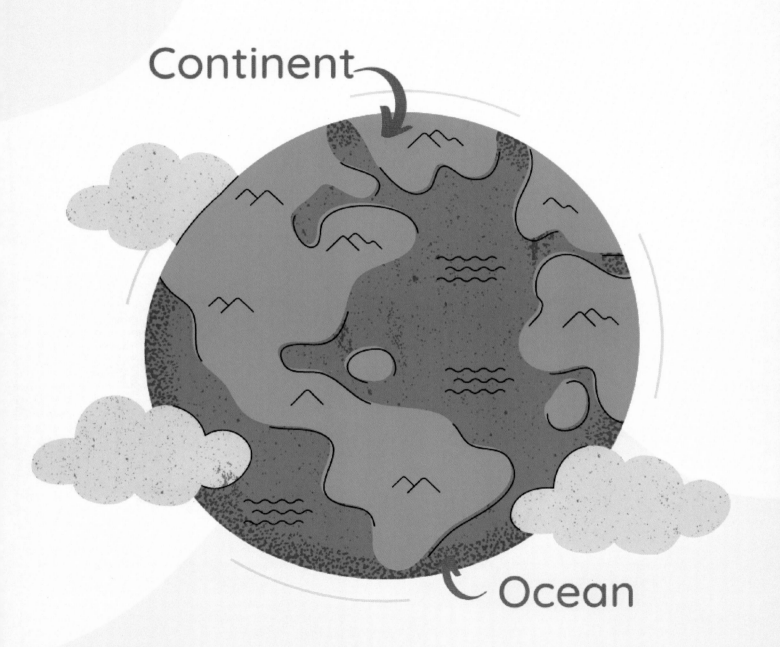

Continent

Ocean

ASIA

Asia is the largest continent on our planet, both in size and population. There are 49 countries in Asia. More than 2300 languages are spoken in Asia.

AFRICA

Africa is the second largest continent in size and the second largest in population. There are 54 countries in Africa. About 2,000 different languages are spoken in Africa.

Nile River

Lion

Pyramid of Giza

Ostrich

Sahara Desert

Elephant

Where in the World ?

NORTH AMERICA

North America is the third largest continent in size and the fourth largest in population. There are 23 countries in North America. English, Spanish and French are the most popular spoken languages in North America.

Chichen Itza

Niagara Falls

Cougar

Eagle

Statue of Liberty

Bison

Where in the World?

SOUTH AMERICA

South America is the fourth largest continent in size and the fifth largest in population. There are 12 countries in South America. Spanish and English are the most widely spoken languages in South America.

Amazon River

Alpaca

Amazon Parrot

Christ the Redeemer

Jaguar

Machu Picchu

Where in the World ?

ANTARTICA

Antarctica is the fifth largest continent in size and is the least populated. Antarctica is a cold icy desert and contains most of our planet's ice and fresh water.

Penguin Colonies

Fur Seal

Deception Island

Penguin

EUROPE

Europe is the second smallest continent in size and the third largest in population. There are 50 countries in Europe and 24 official languages of which the five most spoken native languages are Russian, German, French, Italian, and English.

Eiffel Tower

Leaning Tower of Pisa

Moose

Acropolis of Athens

Greater Spotted Eagle

Eurasian Lynx

Australia

Australia is the smallest continent in size and the sixth largest in population. Australia is the only country in the world that covers an entire continent and is completely surrounded by water. English is the most widely spoken language in Australia.

Uluru

Koala

Kookaburra

Sydney Opera House

The Great Barrier Reef

Kangaroo

Arctic Ocean

Pacific Ocean

Atlantic Ocean

North America

Africa

South America

FIVE OCEANS SURROUNDING THE CONTINENTS

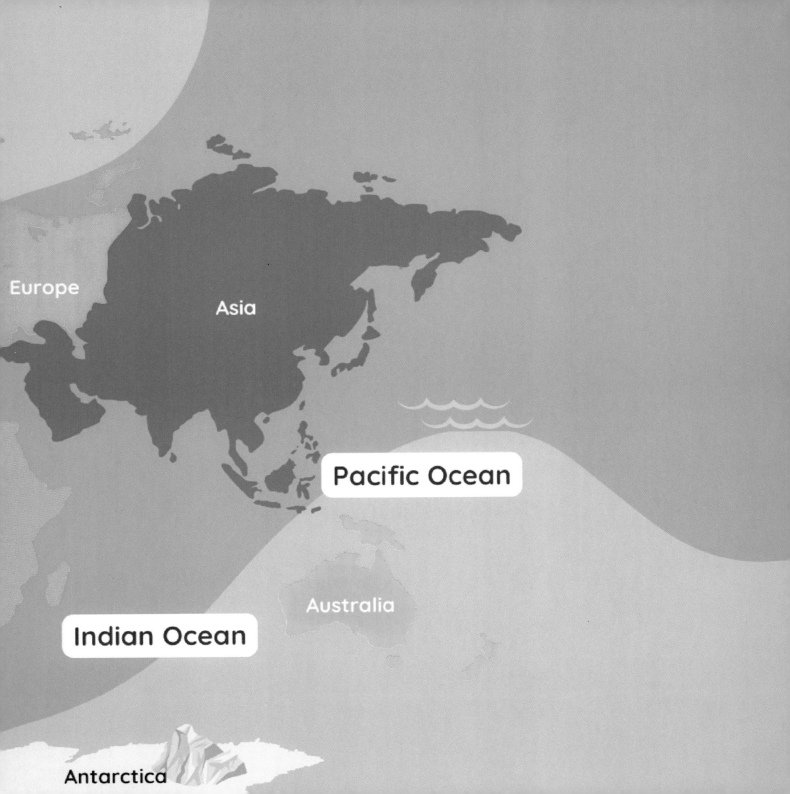

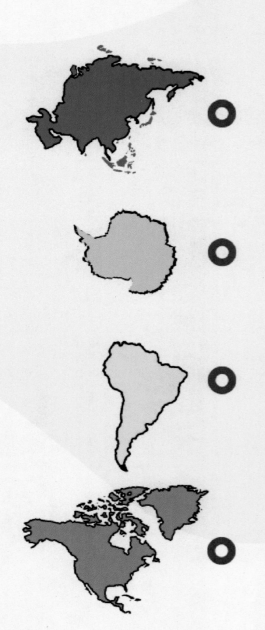

○ ○ ANTARTICA

○ ○ SOUTH AMERICA

○ ○ NORTH AMERICA

○ ○ ASIA

 O

O EUROPE

 O

O AFRICA

 O

O AUSTRALIA

MATCH THE
NAME GAME !

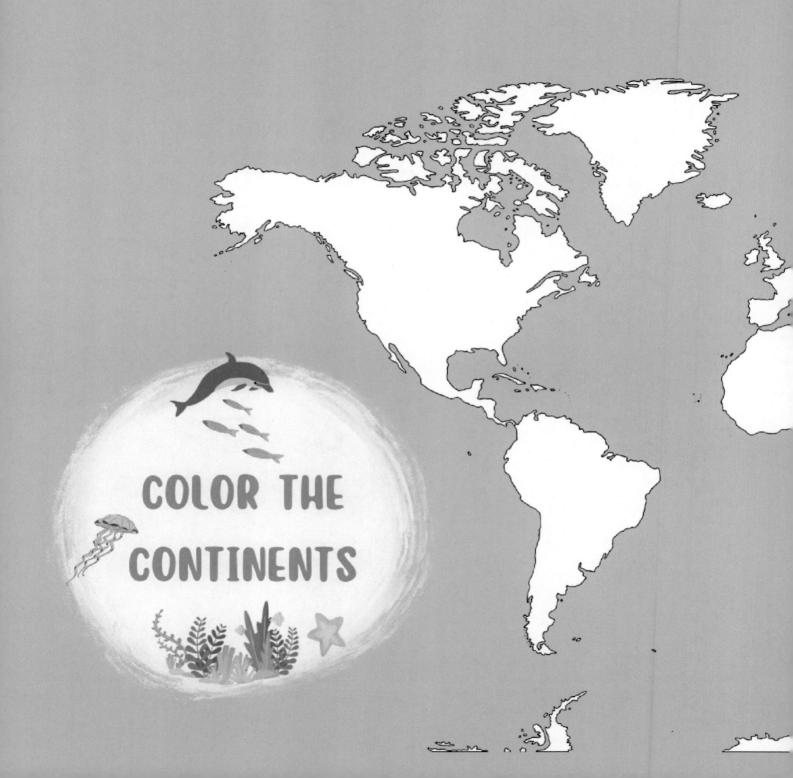

COLOR THE
CONTINENTS

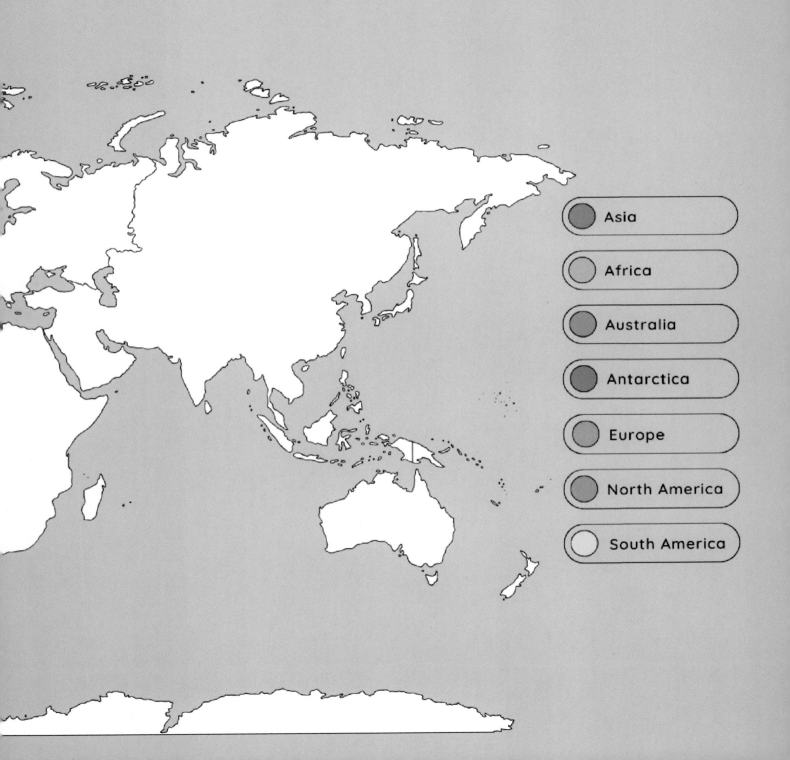

Asia

Africa

Australia

Antarctica

Europe

North America

South America

Made in the USA
Monee, IL
02 October 2022

15054174R00017